CW01010953

Forthcoming titles in this series will include

- *Positive PR*
- *Building Customer Loyalty*
- *Effective Direct Mail*
- *High Performance Sales Management*
- *Win–Win Negotiation*
- *Coping Under Pressure*
- *Mastering Motivation*
- *Getting and Keeping a Positive Attitude*

Do you have ideas for subjects which could be included in this exciting and innovative series? Could your company benefit from close involvement with a forthcoming title?

Please contact David Grant Publishing Limited
80 Ridgeway, Pembury, Tunbridge Wells, Kent TN2 4EZ, UK
Tel/fax +44 (0)1892 822886
Email GRANTPUB@aol.com
with your ideas or suggestions.

SUCCESSFUL
INTERNET MARKETING

60

!

Veronica Yuill

60 Minutes Success Skills Series

Copyright © David Grant Publishing Limited 1999

First published 1999 by
David Grant Publishing Limited
80 Ridgeway
Pembury
Kent TN2 4EZ
United Kingdom

00   99   10 9 8 7 6 5 4 3 2 1

60 Minutes Success Skills Series is an imprint of
David Grant Publishing Limited

All rights reserved. Except for the quotation of short passages for the
purposes of criticism and review, no part of this publication may be
reproduced, stored in a retrieval system, or transmitted, in any form or by
any means, electronic, mechanical, photocopying, recording or
otherwise, without the prior permission of the publisher.

British Library Cataloguing in Publication Data
A CIP catalogue record for this book is available from the British Library

ISBN 1-901306-20-8

Cover design: Liz Rowe
Text design: Graham Rich
Production editor: Paul Stringer

Typeset in Futura by
Archetype IT Ltd, web site http://www.archetype-it.com
Printed and bound in Great Britain by
T.J. International Ltd, Padstow, Cornwall

This book is printed on acid-free paper

*The publishers accept no responsibility for any investment or financial
decisions made on the basis of the information in this book. Readers are advised
always to consult a qualified financial adviser.*

*All names mentioned in the text have been changed to protect the
identity of the business people involved. Any resemblance to existing companies or
people is entirely coincidental.*

CONTENTS

ABOUT *SUCCESSFUL INTERNET MARKETING*

Can you learn to use the Internet as a marketing tool in just one hour? The answer, quite simply, is "YES".

The only bit of waffle in the book

The 60 Minutes Success Skills Series is written for people with neither the time nor the patience to trawl through acres of jargon and page-filling waffle. Like all the books in the series, *Successful Internet Marketing* has been written in the belief that you can learn all you really need to know quickly and without hassle. The aim is to provide essential, practical advice you can use straight away.

Is this book for you?

You don't need to be a nerd, geek, dweeb, or wonk to use this book (although if you are, reading it won't hurt you). It's packed full of useful tips to help you decide how best to market your products and services using the Internet. It's not a technical manual – its aim is to help you unravel all that waffle and hype about the Internet and get down to business.

If you want to know the answers to questions such as:

○ *why should I bother with the Internet?*
○ *what's so special about marketing on the Internet?*
○ *how can I use email to get closer to my customers?*
○ *how do I attract visitors to my Web site?*
○ *what makes an effective Web site?*
○ *can I sell online?*

. . . then this quick, no-bull guide is for you. It's packed with examples which highlight the promises and the pitfalls of marketing in cyberspace.

How to use this book

The message in the 60 Minutes Success Skills Series is "It's OK to skim". Each book is written in a way that allows you to flick through to find the help you most need. This book is a collection of hands-on tips and practical examples which will help you to get your Internet marketing off to a great start, without wasting time and effort rushing up blind alleys. You don't have to read it all in one go or try to put everything into practice right away.

You will find that there are some graphic features used throughout the book:

These features ask you to think about something – they set the scene and prompt you to consider whether particular situations apply to you.

These features give you the framework for an action plan or suggest some research you can do – this will help you to get your own ideas in order.

Where technical terms are unavoidable, these features explain what they mean!

These features appear at the end of each chapter. They are checklists which summarise all the advice given throughout the chapter and are also a useful reminder of what's where when you come back to look at this book in the future. Similar features also appear within chapters which are overflowing with tips.

If you're really pushed for time, you can always go direct to the tips at the end of each chapter.

Contact the author

The Internet is all about connecting people. If you have questions or comments about the contents of this book you can contact the author by email at veronicay@archetype-it.com or visit her Web site, www.archetype-it.com.

What's in this chapter for you

> *What's the Net all about?*
> *Do you need it?*
> *A global marketplace*

What's the Net all about?

> ❝ *It might be easier to get a grasp of what the Internet is all about if there wasn't so much hype. I've had it up to here with people telling me I must have a Web site, that it's going to change the world, that it's the only way to do business. None of these people can give me hard facts to convince me that my business will benefit from the Internet – at any rate not without demanding a fat consultancy fee!* ❞
> **– Vic Targett, MD of a haulage firm**

There is no hype in this book – its aim is to help you decide, without the aid of expensive consultants, whether the Internet can play a worthwhile role in promoting your business. We look at the promises and the pitfalls with the aid of specific examples. If in the end you decide you want to dip your toe in the water, we give you a quick guide to getting connected.

Well, what is it? First of all, the Internet is not just the World Wide Web, although the two terms are often used as if they meant the same thing. It started life in the US Defense Department at the height of the cold war, as a worldwide network of interconnected computers. Later it was adopted by researchers and academics all over the world as a quick and economical way to collaborate on projects and share their findings. It is only in the last few years that it's been used for commercial ends. Its non-commercial origins still show in the vast range of resources that are offered free by Net enthusiasts.

Many people expect to get 'something for nothing' on the Net. If you're going to charge, you had better make your offering pretty special.

To computer buffs, the magical thing about the Internet is that it allows all sorts of different computers to communicate with each other from anywhere in the world, as if they were in the same room, without their users having to know a thing about how it all hangs together. The computers engage in a global game of 'pass the parcel', handing messages on until they arrive at their destination.

Nowadays, the Internet provides a home for:

○ *Electronic mail – used for exchanging everything from simple 'Hi, how are you?' messages to complex three-dimensional simulations*
○ *Newsgroups – global discussion forums covering every topic under the sun and quite a few that aren't*
○ *And, of course, the World Wide Web, the most hyped of all – a system that links words, pictures, sounds and video into a 'Web' of information which you can wander through at will, jumping from one site to the next with a simple mouse-click.*

This book concentrates on these three popular applications. The Internet is also used to transfer files, operate computers remotely, 'chat' online, and increasingly for video conferencing and telephoning as well.

Since the Internet became available for commercial use in 1994, the number of users and networks connected has grown enormously, and continues to do so. Currently more than 50% of users are in the United States, but the rapid rate of growth elsewhere could soon change this.

The two applications which have proved of most use commercially so far are email, and the World Wide Web. Email succeeds because of the ease and convenience with which you can use it to communicate with people all over the world, at very low cost. The Web has liberated the Net from its 'techie' image and made it far more user-friendly by conveying information using colourful graphics and hypertext.

Hypertext: *a system of linking related documents using highlighted words which, when clicked on, call up further information on that topic.*

Browser: *the program on your computer which allows you to view Web pages. The two most common are Microsoft's Internet Explorer, and Netscape Navigator.*

A Web site consists of linked pages of information which can be viewed from anywhere in the world on any computer with an Internet connection and a browser. Originally these pages were purely text but they may now include pictures, sounds, even live video and audio broadcasts. When watching TV, your interaction is limited to zapping with the remote control, or lobbing beer cans at particularly offensive presenters. However, many Web sites give you the possibility of controlling what you see or requesting additional information. For example on your first visit to a news site you could specify what topics interest you. On subsequent visits, relevant headlines would be displayed on the first page. This flexibility makes the Web a very powerful tool for two-way communication between you and your customers.

The technology for creating Web sites is widely available and relatively cheap, so its use has exploded over the last few years. The Web is a mine of information on every conceivable subject, and sites range from 'Joe's Home Page', adorned with pictures of his dogs and children, to Microsoft's vast display of technical expertise and marketing muscle. Of course, if you have big money you can make a bigger splash, but the Internet is all about building communities of common interest; a small business with the right approach can succeed where a larger, more anonymous company might fail.

One of the stumbling blocks to using the Net for commerce is its very openness. Sending highly confidential information? All that email whizzing around the planet is just plain, simple text which can be read by whoever happens to intercept it – from well-intentioned site administrators to determined hackers. Software for encrypting email in order to protect confidentiality is now becoming widely available (although subject to government regulation).

Equally, online commerce is being hampered by the lack of standards for ensuring the security of monetary transactions on the Net. We'll look at this in detail in Chapter 4.

Do you need it?

For most businesses, being on the Internet means having a Web site. At times it seems as if everyone from the mega-corporation to your local corner shop either has a Web site or is considering it. And as Vic Targett has discovered there is no shortage of people willing to convince you to part with your money to set up your own.

If you haven't done so already, get yourself an Internet subscription, and start exploring the Web. It's an essential first step towards deciding whether your company can do business on the Internet.

What can you do with a Web site? The answer depends on what sort of business you are in, your budget – and your imagination.

- You could simply put your brochures, catalogues and price lists on line. A Web site is cheaper and quicker to update than printed materials, and it's available to customers all over the world, all of the time.
- You could add an interactive form, allowing visitors to request information, provide feedback, or place orders.
- You could use the site to improve customer service, providing answers to frequently asked questions, or up-to-date product information.
- You could set up a fully-fledged online shop, allowing customers to input credit card details and have the goods delivered to their door.
- For some types of business, a Web site can provide real competitive advantage. For example, Fedex's Web site allows customers to track the progress of their packages in real time by typing in the consignment number.

Even if you think a Web site is not for you, think about the other less glamorous applications of the Internet. Could you use email to speed up communications with suppliers, for example? Or consider using the Web as a vast reference library the next time you need to track down some elusive piece of useful information.

> ❝ *I've seen other people spending a fortune on flashy Web sites, and it hasn't made a penny difference to their sales. Let them waste their money if they want – we're doing very nicely without, thanks!* ❞
> **– Adrian Scott-Edwards, estate agent**

You shouldn't necessarily be put off by the bad experiences of others – often failure can be put down to lack of planning, an inappropriate product, and/or poor design. Little does Adrian know that a million-pound villa on the Côte d'Azur was sold within twenty minutes via the Internet! In some businesses, *not* having an Internet presence could soon put you at a serious disadvantage. There's no need to spend a fortune either – the cost of access has dropped enough for even small businesses to present a professional image on the Net. A well thought out Web site can be a cost-effective way of building your image, finding new customers, and providing a better service for your existing ones.

> None of your competitors has a Web site? It's a great chance to get in there first and make an impact. But do make sure you have a clear idea of what you hope to achieve with the site before you start.

A global marketplace

> 66 *When I first started using the Internet, it seemed to be entirely populated by nerds and techies. It's changed a lot since it became a mass medium. Now it's become just another place to do business.* 99
> **– Peter Leadbetter, online gardening supplies retailer**

It's easy to become mesmerised by the technology of the Internet, all those computerised bells and whistles. Don't! Just think of it as another marketplace for your products and services. You don't always need the latest and greatest gadgetry to make a good impression – some very successful business ventures on the Internet were launched using plain, unadorned text. The key, as always, is to listen to your customers.

> 66 *The fantastic thing about the Internet is that it allows you to communicate one-to-one across the globe. You can very easily collect information about your customers and provide them with customised information that addresses their needs. No other medium allows you to do this so cheaply.* 99
> **– Will Forester, Internet marketing consultant**

In short, if you do business nationally or internationally – or would like to – and if your target markets have access to and use the

Net, you should be seriously considering establishing yourself on the Internet.

Assessing the Internet from your point of view

1. Establish realistic goals for your Internet ventures, and be prepared to adapt your strategy if things don't go according to plan.
2. Be focused – define your target market and don't try to be all things to all men.
3. Look at your Internet presence from the point of view of your customers, and seek to provide genuinely useful services which are of value to them.
4. Be prepared to offer something for nothing.
5. You don't need to spend an arm and a leg to get going on the Internet – you can start small and build your presence gradually.
6. If you're a small business, you can use your Web site to make you look bigger than you are.
7. Many Internet applications (such as email and the World Wide Web) allow you to build one-to-one relationships with customers in a way that is difficult with other media.

What's in this chapter for you

To spam or not to spam?
'Opt-in' mailing lists and newsletters
Newsgroups (online forums)
Dealing with incoming email effectively

Email really is the 'killer tool' on the Internet. Web sites may be more glamorous, but email gets the job done, day in day out. Anyone who has used it for more than a few months soon finds it as essential as the telephone (if not more so). If only for this reason, it has to be considered as part of your marketing armoury. This chapter introduces the ways that email and related tools can be used to build up your online presence.

To spam or not to spam?

> ❝ *I sent out an email to my friend's mailing list of about three hundred names launching my new online business. I was amazed to get back twenty rude replies telling me I had no right to spam them. I sent apologies, but it really shocked me that I offended them. We get junk mail in the post every day. Okay, we throw most of it out, but sometimes we see a great offer, and we make a purchase. Why do people get so wound up about bulk email?* ❞
> **– Peter Leadbetter, online gardening supplies retailer**

At first sight, email looks like a golden opportunity for direct mail. You compose your sales pitch, select your mailing list, and send out ten, twenty, or a thousand letters in minutes, for the same as it would cost you to send a single message! If you've had an email account for a while, you have almost certainly received some 'Unsolicited commercial email' (less politely referred to as 'Spam' – allegedly in reference to a renowned Monty Python sketch where everything on the menu was the same: Spam!). Much of it is of the 'Make Money Fast!' pyramid selling variety. Some of it offers software to allow you to do your very own spamming. Some is more subtle. Some you may even find interesting.

If you received this type of email, what would your reaction to it be? Would you be amused, bored, annoyed, or downright furious? Would you ever make a purchase, or just visit a Web site as a result of an unsolicited email?

It may seem to you that getting rid of unwanted email is as simple as pressing the delete key. Certainly it's a lot easier than getting rid of a pushy salesman with his foot in the door. But 'spam' has had a very bad press on the Internet. In short, some people get very angry about it.

> 66 Today, I had to delete 16 unwanted messages from my in-box. It costs me money to download this junk, and it costs me time to deal with it. The targeting is pathetic – why should I be interested in marrying an attractive Russian lady? On principle I will never deal with a company that behaves in this way. 99
> – Lorraine Marks, freelance financial consultant

On the other hand, if people carry on doing it, it must work, right? Just as with 'junk' mail you receive in the post, even if only 1% of recipients take up the offer, that can mean a lot of business for the sender. He or she may not care about the 10% (or whatever) of irate recipients.

However, not everyone reacts as coolly as Lorraine. It's quite common for Internet users to:

- bombard the mailbox of the sender with messages until it is full
- email the sender's Internet provider asking for their account to be closed
- publish the details of the sender on an anti-spam Web site.

None of these is good for your image, and the first and second could result very quickly in lost business, if important emails go astray. Some bulk emailers use fake or free email addresses to avoid these problems – hardly a good way to induce confidence in your business.

So what's to be done? It seems a shame to pass up a golden opportunity to put your sales message right on the desktop of your potential customer. Part of the problem is that Internet direct mail is still in its infancy. If you have used conventional direct mail you will know that you can hire or buy lists of names and addresses according to very specific criteria. *Not* using targeted lists would be considered a waste of time and money. On the Internet, it is as yet very difficult to obtain categorised lists of email addresses – and, in addition, using a scattergun approach is not significantly more expensive than targeting. However, more sensitive Internet marketers who do not wish to be seen as 'spammers' use alternative approaches.

> ❝ *'Mass market' approaches certainly have their place on the Net – but I feel that, just as on dry land, you get the biggest bang for your buck using targeted direct response techniques. Know your customers! As always this is the key to successful marketing.* ❞
> **– Will Forester, Internet marketing consultant**

If you decide to use bulk email, minimise the risk of being seen as a 'spammer'.

- ❏ *Always include a valid return address and contact details.*
- ❏ *Provide an option to refuse further correspondence. If someone asks to be removed from the list, do so.*
- ❏ *Don't use a free email service or you will be seen as a spammer. Many people use 'spam filters' which automatically reject mail from these services, so your carefully honed message will never be seen.*
- ❏ *Put your message across in a paragraph or two maximum. Don't burble on for pages and pages. If you make your key points effectively, your prospect will take the next step and ask for more information.*
- ❏ *Put the point of the message in the first line.*
- ❏ *If anyone sends you email accusing you of spamming, take a deep breath and get on with your life. Don't be tempted to fire back an angry retort.*

'Opt-in' mailing lists and newsletters

> ❝ *We struck gold by providing an option on our Web site to sign up for an occasional email newsletter giving details of special offers and new arrivals. To make it more attractive, we include seasonal tips, and subscribers are offered discounts on featured products.*

We had over 100 subscribers within the first month, and traffic on the site shoots up for the two or three days after the mailing goes out. **"**
– Peter Leadbetter

Peter's subscribers are a marketer's dream – all of them have expressed interest in his products beyond simply browsing his site. They have taken the time to fill in a form on his site, and have trusted him with their email addresses.

'Opt-in' mailing lists are the latest fashion in Internet marketing. What could be simpler? Just provide a box to enter an email address and a 'Subscribe' button on your Web site, and you can build up your own list of people who are happy to receive email from you. If you sell a product or service that invites repeat business, keeping in touch with your customers via a newsletter is the best way to get more sales. It's more work than mass mailshots, but for your product or service it may be more appropriate, and more effective.

Here are some things to consider at the planning stage:

- ❑ *What's in it for them? People won't sign up for a straight sales pitch – the mailing must contain information which is of value to them.*
- ❑ *Reward your subscribers for their trust with exclusive special offers or loyalty schemes.*
- ❑ *You could use the opportunity to gather extra information about your customers by asking them to fill in additional details – where they live, or their age for example. But beware: some Internet users have an attention span too short to fill in more than their email address. And some may object to providing this information. So it should always be optional.*
- ❑ *Make sure you provide a simple way to unsubscribe from the list as well!*
- ❑ *Keep the mailing list to yourself. And reassure subscribers that you will not pass on their addresses to others.*
- ❑ *The software you use to send mass emails should not allow recipients to see the other addresses on the list. It's not a smart move to give away your list of potential customers.*

" We made our database of members available online; it was in a 'members only' section of the Web site which requires a password to access it. We thought this was secure enough, but recently our members have been complaining that they have received emails from a competing company soliciting their business. It seems someone from this company signed up with us for the sole purpose of stealing our customers' contact information. "
– Sally Webster, customer service manager

Think about what you could usefully provide to your actual and potential customers in an email newsletter. It need not contain any straight 'selling' at all; you could simply provide information that is of value to them. This will build up your reputation and establish a relationship of trust (assuming your information is reliable, of course).

" Most people will not buy the first time they see your sales message, nor the second or even the third time. You have to keep your name and services in front of your prospects constantly (most marketers reckon on at least seven times) to make the best sales. Plus, the Internet is a community of co-operation and exchange of information. If you've helped someone in the past, chances are they'll remember your name, and come to you when they want to buy. "
– Andy Toklas, freelance Web designer

Is your product or service suitable for a newsletter-type approach? If so, do you have the resources to maintain one? If you don't, can you rent a targeted list of email addresses from an online marketing firm for one-off mailings? Or, could you advertise in an existing email newsletter aimed at your target market? Remember to check out the credentials of the firm carefully though, or the results may not be as good as you hoped.

Newsgroups (online forums)

You may have heard of 'Usenet News' – a network of thousands of online newsgroups (discussion forums) covering pretty much every topic under the sun, from the serious to the frankly ridiculous (*alt.chips.salt-n-vinegar*, anyone?). With the appropriate software, anyone can read or contribute to these newsgroups. Among many other things, people use them to:

- *argue about sex, politics, and religion*
- *swop recipes*
- *give and receive advice on resolving technical problems*
- *provide support for people suffering from serious illness or disability*
- *and, not unpredictably, exchange pornographic images.*

They sound like a great idea (except for the last one!), and certainly some of them can be an excellent source of advice, information, and support. However, visiting a few groups will quickly reveal disadvantages. The vast majority of these groups are not 'moderated' – i.e. there is no quality control over what is posted there.

- *Information given may be misleading or plain wrong.*
- *You may have to wade through scores of messages which are not relevant to the topic.*
- *In some groups, 'flaming' (posting rude, abusive messages) is quite common – often in response to some naive person sending what others consider to be an inappropriate message.*

> If you had an Internet account, you could try visiting a few newsgroups covering topics that interest you, and judge for yourself the quality of what you find there.

You may find a newsgroup which seems an ideal place to find potential customers for your product. For example, if you sell exercise wear, *misc.fitness.aerobic* may seem like an excellent place to post a message promoting your products. Unfortunately, this approach suffers from the same set of problems as bulk email. Hardened Usenet users consider the Internet to be a hallowed place free from commerce and will promptly bombard with 'flames' anyone posting a straight advert to a newsgroup. So a more subtle approach is necessary.

> " *I have several newsgroups about graphic arts and Web design that I regularly visit. I always sign off my messages with my website address, contact details, and my company slogan. It costs me nothing, and it's another way of getting my name in front of possible customers. It's a useful starting point for networking too.* "
> **– Andy Toklas**

Of course, subtlety isn't everything. If you believe that your product can genuinely help to solve someone's problem, then say so.

Get the most from newsgroups:

- ❏ *Before posting to an unfamiliar group, 'lurk' for a while (i.e. read without contributing) to get an idea of the tone of the group. There may also be a 'FAQ' (Frequently Asked Questions list) – if there is, read it. It may save embarrassment later.*
- ❏ *Contribute useful, informative postings and people will recognise you as an authority. If you recommend your own product, declare your interest.*
- ❏ *If you contribute regularly to newsgroups, create a 'signature file' with your contact details in it. You can set up your software to attach it automatically to each message that you post.*
- ❏ *After you've posted to newsgroups for a while, you may notice an increase in the amount of 'junk email' you receive. 'Hoovering' email addresses from newsgroups is a favoured practice of bulk emailers.*

After visiting a few, you may decide that newsgroups are not for you. However, if it is appropriate for your product, there is nothing to stop you setting up your own discussion forum on your Web site. There are various ready-made software packages for Web-based discussions available, many requiring little or no expertise to install and configure. This can provide an opportunity to collect valuable customer feedback and ideas for product improvements.

People may also post negative comments which will be displayed for all to see. How you are going to deal with these?

> " *We set up a forum on our site for tech support, with a 'frequently asked questions' list. Customers could often find a solution to their problem simply by visiting the forum. In addition, they could help each other out. It's a valuable service for them and it cut down phone calls to our support department by 20%!* "
> **– Jennifer Dalglish, helpdesk manager for a software company**

As with newsletters, you could require registration for your forum, thus enabling you to gather further information about your customers. You should also allocate some time to managing the forum, 'seeding' it with messages to get it going if necessary, and removing inappropriate postings.

Dealing with incoming email effectively

> " *Since we started publishing our Web site and email addresses in all our publicity, my department gets 50 to 60 emails a day. We didn't expect it, and we were just swamped. I nearly lost an important customer because we had no system for prioritising the incoming mail, and an urgent message went unanswered for two days!* "
> **– Sally Webster**

Once the Internet is part of your company culture, it will certainly change the way you do business. You need to be prepared for the consequences, and plan ahead to avoid problems like Sally's. In practice, the volume of email usually builds up slowly, giving you time to adjust – but you may need to reorganise in order to handle it promptly and efficiently.

Make sure your staff are trained in the effective use of their email software. If necessary, establish company standards for presentation and response times – just as you would do for letters and telephone calls. Remember, every email sends a message about the professionalism of your company.

Change your culture

- ❑ *Get staff to set up standard 'signature files' to add to messages, to save time and ensure consistency. You can also use these signatures to highlight promotions or new products.*
- ❑ *Set up 'generic' mailboxes such as 'support@yourcompany.com' or 'sales@yourcompany.com'. Checking and responding to messages to these addresses can be rotated among staff to cover for holidays and absences. But make sure everyone knows whose turn it is.*
- ❑ *For standard information requests, you can set up an 'autoresponder' which automatically replies to the email with a prefabricated message, leaving staff free to deal with more specific requests.*

Remember, email is just another way of communicating. If your customers prefer to use email, you will get fewer phone calls and faxes, allowing you to reallocate resources. And email is less intrusive than the phone.

> ❝ *In the end, someone from our IT department showed me the 'filter' option in the email software. It sorts the incoming mail according to who it's from, or the text in the subject line. I created appropriate folders for each category of email, and now email from my key customers automatically gets filed in 'urgent'! It can even forward important messages to my assistant when I'm absent. It saves me and my staff time, and it ensures that important items don't get overlooked.* ❞
> **– Sally Webster**

Make the most of email

1. If you decide to use email as a marketing tool, tread carefully and target as accurately as you can.
2. Consider using an email newsletter or occasional briefing to keep in touch with your customers.
3. If it's appropriate for your product, provide an interactive discussion area on your Web site to encourage feedback and problem-solving.

4. Read previous messages before posting to an unfamiliar newsgroup, to find out whether it's an appropriate place for your message.

5. Set up a 'standard signature' for emails and newsgroup messages with all your contact information and, if relevant, a key slogan about your product.

6. Keep mailing lists confidential, and tell members so. If you are going to sell the list, say so up front!

7. Make sure all your staff are trained and aware of targets for answering email.

8. Ensure you have adequate resources for managing forums and mailing lists.

What's in this chapter for you

Creating and promoting a Web site
Getting traffic to your site – and keeping it
What makes an effective Web site?

The Web is certainly the most visible part of the Internet – and also the part surrounded by the most hype. Unfortunately it's also the place where many have come to grief! In this chapter we'll identify the pitfalls, and give some pointers to creating and maintaining a successful Web site.

Creating and promoting a Web site

❝ *The number one reason people visit Web sites is for information. You have to give people a benefit for visiting your site. I find many new clients don't fully understand this – they just want to put a straight sales pitch online. That won't cut it on the Web, and I'm not afraid to say so.* ❞
– Andy Toklas, freelance Web designer

Before you even start on your Web site, put yourself in your customers' shoes and ask yourself some hard questions:

○ *What makes your business special?*
○ *What's in it for the customer?*
○ *Is your site worth coming back to?*

Let's look at these questions in turn. They may not be as simple as they seem. After asking these questions, you might even decide that a Web site is not appropriate for your business, or that you are not yet prepared to allocate resources to maintaining one.

What makes your business special?

Yes, it's your 'USP – Unique Selling Point'. If you haven't got one, or don't know what it is, you should! Identify it, and make it the key to your site. But make sure it's not something vague like 'lowest prices' or 'best widgets' – it needs to be specific and backed up with evidence.

> ❝ *Definitely no waffle on the front page! It should state clearly what product or service you are offering, and what the benefit is to the customer. How will it help them? Why do they need it? It's so easy for people to surf off somewhere else – you've got to grab their attention fast.* ❞
> **– Will Forester, Internet marketing consultant**

What's in it for the customer?

As Andy says, you must provide a benefit for your visitors. Not only has the site got to look good and present a professional image, it has to provide hard information. 'Content is king!' is a mantra on the Web. This doesn't have to be anything huge or complicated, but you should be able to think of something suitable. Be prepared to give away something for free. It's the starting point for building up a relationship with your visitors.

Think of your customer's interests when writing copy, not your own. Don't waffle on about how great your product is – talk about their needs, and how your product fulfils them.

Is your site worth coming back to?

> ❝ *To keep our site fresh-looking we change the front page at least every month, highlighting special offers and seasonal gardening tips. Sure, it's a lot of work, but it definitely pays for itself in repeat visits – and sales.* ❞
> **– Peter Leadbetter, online gardening supplies retailer**

If you want to do business on the Web, you need people to return to your site, and spread the word about it to others. For one thing, most people won't make a buying decision on their first visit. And if you look at 'off-Web' marketing, exactly the same principles apply. Large companies don't go on showing the same television adverts year after year – people would get bored with them if they did. If your site remains unchanged month in month out, people will stop returning. And eventually you will run out of new visitors to keep the flow of traffic up!

Good design and planning pays dividends

- ❑ *When planning your web site, make sure you budget for the ongoing work of keeping it up-to-date.*
- ❑ *The design of the site should make updates and additions as easy as possible – otherwise they won't get done.*
- ❑ *Link directly to new items from the front page (for example with a 'What's new' icon) so that visitors can see immediately what has changed since their last visit.*

Do some research on the Web. If your competitors have Web sites, visit them and look at them with a critical eye.

- ○ *What do you like about them?*
- ○ *What don't you like?*
- ○ *How can you make yours stand out?*

You must have answers to these questions before you put pen to paper (or finger to keyboard) to start designing your site. A serious Web designer should certainly ask you these questions, or ones very like them, before starting work. But they are equally important if you are doing it yourself.

Brainstorm the purpose of your site, as well as its main selling points. Then try to distil out the essence of your site into a single short paragraph. If you can't do this, your site will lack focus.

Getting traffic to your site – and keeping it

> **"** *I read recently that there are something like 300 million pages on the Web. It's an awesome thought! How are people ever going to find my little Web site among all the rest?* **"**
> **– Nicholas Jeffreys, jeweller**

You can spend months creating the perfect Web site – but if no-one knows about it all that effort will be wasted and your masterpiece will languish in a dusty, unvisited corner of the Web!

In this section you'll learn the main ways of publicising your Web site.

Before you start to promote your site, it has to be as good as you can make it.

- ❏ *Check and re-check to make sure there are no errors, spelling mistakes, or links that don't work.*
- ❏ *Get friends or colleagues to review it and provide constructive criticism.*

There's nothing worse than finally putting your site on line and instead of congratulations receiving sour emails pointing out your mistakes.

Remember: you only get one chance to make a first impression!

Search engines

❝ *The sources of your site's traffic will evolve as your site matures. At first, you need to rely heavily on search engines and directories to get visitors. As time goes on, you will find less fickle sources of visitors, and your dependence on search engines will decrease. But to start with, they are vital.* ❞
– Andy Toklas

A **search engine** is a gigantic online index of Web pages. Visitors type in key words or a question to describe what they are looking for (for example 'cheap flights to Majorca') and the engine displays a list of results in order of relevance. Clicking on one of these takes you to the relevant site.

Search engines have to be the first port of call when promoting your Web site – simply because they are the first place most people go when they are looking for information on the Web. So you must go through the grind of submitting your site to all the major search engines and directories such as Yahoo!, Alta Vista, and Infoseek. You can pay others to do it for you, or use one of the Web-based services that allows you to fill in the relevant information on one screen, and then sends it to all of the major engines to save you retyping it each time.

> **"** *I considered using a submission service, but in the end I did it myself. At the time I did it to save money, but I think it was worth doing in any case. I know my products best, and I was able to make sure the site got listed in the correct categories and under the right keywords.* **"**
> **– Peter Leadbetter**

Don't forget that there may be smaller specialist search sites dedicated to your speciality – for example, if you are a travel agent, there are specialist travel sites you could submit it to.

Submission to search engines is a whole mini-industry in itself, with too many fine points to go into here. Unfortunately, getting your site into the major indexes is only the first step. If your site doesn't come up within the first couple of screens of results for your keywords, it might as well not be there at all – few people will look that far. There are numerous newsgroups, mailing lists and Web sites dedicated to endless discussion of the best ways to ensure a good listing in search engines. A serious professional Web designer should be aware of the requirements and build 'search-engine friendliness' into the site.

Identify the most important words and phrases you think people will use to find your site, and make sure they figure frequently in your copy – without making it sound stilted or repetitive of course!

The most obvious keywords aren't necessarily the best – they might result in millions of results, making it all the harder for you to get to the top of the list. Generally, the more specific the better. If you're unfamiliar with search engines, read their help pages to understand the criteria they use.

Web servers keep a detailed log of every visit to your pages. These can be fed into analysis software which can tell you exactly what visitors typed into the search engines to find you. This can be very helpful in fine-tuning your site to meet your customers' needs.

Web server: *the computer which stores your Web pages. It might be on your own premises, or hosted by a third party.*

You need to revisit search engines every now and then to check your listing hasn't disappeared or slipped down the list.

❝ *It was hopeless trying to get even close to the top of the pile using just the keywords 'secretarial services'. But adding the names of the software packages I use, or the name of my town, narrows it down. So I optimised my pages for a combination of those keywords. It seems to work. I get plenty of visitors coming from Yahoo! and Infoseek.* ❞
– Alice Williams, freelance secretary

Banner exchanges

If you've spent any time on the Web, you will have seen 'banner ads' – the colourful rectangular blocks advertising other sites on the Web, usually bedecked with enticing invitations such as 'Free!' or 'Click here!' Often, but not always, they are related to the content of the page you are looking at. For example if you search for 'French wine' in Yahoo!, you may get a banner on the results page advertising an online wine merchant. So they can be an effective form of promotion. The cost of a banner on a major site like Yahoo! may be prohibitive for a fledgling business. But you don't have to pay a penny to sign up with a 'banner exchange'.

How do they work? Simply put, you agree to display advertisements for other members of the exchange on your site. In return, for every two banners you display, your own banner is displayed once on another site. The whole thing is administered automatically by the banner exchange – all you have to do is design and submit your own banner, and include some special code on one or more of the pages on your site. The exchange also allows you to view statistics showing the number of visitors and your 'click-through rate'.

Click-through rate: *the ratio of the number of people who clicked on your banner to the number of times it was displayed.*

Getting the best from banners

- ❏ *Banner design is an art of its own – you have very little space to get your message across. If you feel you're lacking in graphic design skills, pay a designer specialising in banner ads to do it for you.*
- ❏ *Find a banner exchange that allows you to categorise your site by subject and thus display your banner on other related sites. This is particularly important if you operate in a small niche market.*
- ❏ *Don't expect miracles from banner ad promotion. A click-through rate of about 35:1 is considered quite good.*
- ○ *Don't go overboard with banners on your site in order to increase the number of times your own banner is displayed. They can detract from the appearance of your site – and what's more, when people click on them, they leave!*

❝ *Use banners as an image tool. To make the most of every exposure, develop a coherent visual style that people will recognize as yours. This could be as simple as using the same background colour every time. If you have a logo, always use it. Even if people don't click on it, you'll benefit from the exposure.* ❞
– Will Forester

You can also pay for advertising on specific sites. In this case you will have much more control over the placement of your banner. Costs are normally quoted as 'CPM' (cost per thousand impressions).

Other types of site promotion

> " *I've found that one of the best and cheapest ways to get qualified traffic to my site is to exchange links. If I come across another site that appeals to my target market I email the webmaster asking if they'll link to my site if I link to theirs. I've almost always had a positive response. Needless to say, I don't link to direct competitors' sites!* "
>
> **– Peter Leadbetter**

You may not get much traffic from reciprocal links but it is very likely that people following these links are interested in your product or service.

Can you see the possible benefits of going in for reciprocal linking in a big way? You may even end up with a large collection of related links which in itself is useful to your visitors and will encourage them to return to your site.

Don't forget the conventional offline ways of promoting your business – they can be used equally well to promote your site.

- *Press releases: naturally you will issue one to announce the launch of your site! But news about the site can also be incorporated in other press releases.*
- *Newspaper and magazine ads should always include the address of your site.*
- *Letterheads, compliments slips, business cards – in fact anything printed that leaves your company – should include your web address.*
- *If you use direct mail, offer customers the option of responding via a Web-based form or email, as well as by reply card or telephone.*

Remember that your Web site is just part of your overall marketing strategy. For maximum effect, combine offline and online promotion.

What makes an effective Web site?

> *" The most important thing to get right at the outset is the site's purpose. Why is it there? To inform? To sell? To promote? The answer to this question will dictate the design of the site. I see far too many sites that don't even seem to have asked this question – in the worst cases you wade through three or four pages before you even find out exactly what the product or service is. "*
> **– Will Forester**

The 'online brochure'

A low-budget site can be built simply by reproducing the content of printed brochures and catalogues on line. But think carefully before you do this – what works in print doesn't necessarily work on the Web. As we've noted before, straight selling copy doesn't attract attention, or repeat visits. Nevertheless, you can build an effective site purely on the basis of providing information about your product, service, or company, with very few interactive elements.

Remember: 'content is king'! If you're on a low budget, put most of your effort into producing useful, relevant, and up-to-date content, not flashy design.

> *" There were a few ideas that worked for me. Putting up a purely informative page about gold and silver jewellery – things like an explanation of different grades of precious metals and stones; having a 'what's new' page which is updated regularly with special offers; giving sources of outside information via a links page. It might open the door to competition, but it offers visitors a valuable service and gives them another reason to visit. None of this costs me very much and it's enough to make the site more than a simple catalogue. "*
> **– Nicholas Jeffreys**

Style versus substance

Because Web site creation tools are so accessible, it's tempting to just throw a site together yourself.

❝ Okay, content is king. I know my products best, so I can write the copy. And I don't need a designer – I can just use a couple of shareware software packages and create the site myself. ❞
– Geoff Service, freelance programmer

Up to a point, Geoff! If you are clear about the message you want get across to your target market and you are prepared to spend some time browsing the Web to see what works and what doesn't, you may be able to design an attractive, easy-to-use Web site. After all, many other people who are not professional designers have done just this. On the other hand . . .

❝ Too many DIY sites just scream 'amateur'! Three or four different fonts on one page, horrible flashing graphics downloaded from some freeware site, huge fuzzy pictures that take an age to download, pink text on a blue background. It's hardly going to entice people to spend money on your product. ❞
– Andy Toklas

If you wish to DIY:

❏ *Don't underestimate the time it will take. You'll need to cost your time (or that of your employees) appropriately.*
❏ *If you don't have design experience, find a site that you like the look of and use it as a model for your own (without copying wholesale, of course).*
❏ *Keep it simple, at least to start with. You can always add extra features later.*
❏ *Use the resources available to you on the Internet. There are many newsletters, mailing lists, and Web sites that will help you out with site design.*
❏ *Consider using professionals for specific tasks – e.g. designing logos or banners. This will help to give your site a more polished look.*

Remember, visitors to your site are looking for information. Its purpose should be immediately obvious, and it should be easy to navigate. Great content is no good if they can't find it.

❝ I hate those sites that try so hard to be 'cool', with groovy graphics and 'interesting' page layout. Sure, they've used a skilled

designer, but the site seems to be more about letting the designers show how clever they are than helping me to find what I want. 99
– Lorraine Marks, freelance financial consultant

Look at the sites you visit most often. What is it about them that makes them attractive and/or useful to you? Does the design support or detract from the content?

A site that is glitzy and glamorous may attract people for a short while. But if the content isn't useful they won't come back. It's worth noting that some of the most visited sites on the Web, such as Yahoo!, have a very simple and functional interface. The design serves the purpose of making the content accessible.

One of the great attractions of the Web is the ability to use colourful images – unlike print advertising it costs no more than black and white. You can even make the images move, just by selecting a few options in your graphics software. So it's easy to create lively looking pages.

66 *On my first site, I had a lovely colour picture of the garden centre filling the first page. You could click on different areas depending on what products you were interested in. I thought it looked great – until I visited my parents, proudly showed it off to them, and found that on their computer it took three minutes to download! "World-Wide-Wait, more like," said my dad! Looking at sites like Yahoo! I realised they could make their pages look interesting and colourful just by using a few well-designed small graphics.* 99
– Peter Leadbetter

The trouble with images is that they tend to be large, and many people have a slow connection to the Net. If people have to wait too long for your page to appear, they'll get bored and go elsewhere. Many graphics programs designed for the Web tell you how long a given picture will take to download at different speeds, and provide various options for reducing the file size without affecting the quality.

TIPS

More on the design:

- ❑ *If using a designer, provide a clear brief of exactly what the site is intended to achieve. Be clear about how the designer's proposals will advance your goals.*
- ❑ *Don't require visitors to download additional software ('browser plugins') simply in order to view your site. Any material requiring plugins should be an optional extra.*
- ❑ *Don't strand your visitors in a dead end! Every page on your site should have a link at least to the home page, and to other related pages as well.*
- ❑ *If the site is large and complex, a site map or search facility may help visitors find their way quickly to what they want.*

Adding value

Try to think of ways you can use a Web site to provide something extra for your customers, that could not easily be provided any other way. Web sites are great for:

- ○ *providing up-to-date news, product information, and pricing*
- ○ *asking for feedback*
- ○ *offering free samples, providing this is appropriate for your product or service*
- ○ *niche marketing – with a little effort you can let visitors personalise what they see according to their interests*
- ○ *interactive features – for example online discussion forums*
- ○ *instant, automatic processing of sales and information requests.*

As you move away from the 'online brochure' you can use the Web to meet the needs of individual customers in a much more personal way.

Getting information about actual and potential customers

Not only can your customers get something extra from a Web site – so can you! Used carefully, a Web site can provide an opportunity to get to know your customers far better.

> ❝ *Lots of people are concerned about privacy on the net – will someone grab my email address, are my credit card details safe? But I find that if you actually ask people to give you information by means of a feedback form, a surprising number are willing to give it!* ❞
> **– Peter Leadbetter**

You may work for hours to create, refine, and promote your site. But how do you know it's what your customers want? Ask them. A carefully designed online questionnaire asking for your customers' opinions and suggestions can provide very valuable information which will help you to improve your offer.

It's always best to ask specific questions rather than simply providing a box for general comments. Provide an outlet for constructive criticism. Don't say: 'What did you like about our site?' Ask: 'Was it easy to find the information you were looking for? If not, why not?' Keep your questionnaire brief – especially if you do not offer any kind of reward for filling it in.

> ❝ When I first started out, I increased the number of visits my site attracted from a mere 25 a week to over 500 a week in less than a month by analysing and acting on the information I found in my server log files. ❞
> — **Peter Leadbetter**

All Web servers maintain a log file of accesses. With this file and a software package for analysing it, you can find out quite a lot about your visitors without asking them anything. For example:

- ○ *Exactly where they came from (e.g. a search engine, a link from another site)*
- ○ *What they typed into the search engine*
- ○ *How long they spent on the site and what pages they looked at, in what order*
- ○ *What country they are in.*

Of course, you can also calculate global visitor numbers and trends – useful for convincing others of the effectiveness of your Web site.

> ❝ Use log files to make your web site work, and attract new customers. Looking at the paths people took through the site convinced me that the navigation wasn't clear enough. Since then, I've redesigned my site: my page-view to visitor ratio has doubled and my sale to visitor ratio has increased as well. ❞
> — **Peter Leadbetter**

Customer service and support

You can use your Web site to provide customer service 24 hours a day, seven days a week. Simply providing online product documentation or samples, and up-to-date prices, can reduce calls to customer service, and promote the image of your company.

> Ask your customer service staff to document the most frequently asked questions. Then post the answers on your Web site.

❝ Since we put our Web site up, we've found that not only do we get fewer calls, but 70% of the customers who do call have gathered information from the Web site first. So calls are shorter and more effective. ❞

– Sally Webster

The do's and dont's of site design

1. Put yourself in your customers' shoes when designing your Web site. Provide information that's useful to them.
2. Make the purpose of your Web site clear from the first page.
3. When planning the site, budget for regular updates to keep it fresh.
4. Remember that 'content is king!', and allocate resources accordingly.
5. Consider the requirements of search engines when writing copy for the Web.
6. Ask for comments and criticism – from friends, colleagues, and customers – and use them to improve your site.
7. Use your Web site to provide something extra for your customers, that could not easily be provided any other way.
8. If in doubt, KISS (Keep it Simple, Stupid!)

What's in this chapter for you

Is it right for your product?
Can you afford it?
Setting standards
Can you make a go of an Internet-only business?

In this chapter we look at using the Internet not just to promote your company and its products, but actually for online selling, using a Web site to display the products and collect the cash. There's a lot of hype at present about 'e-commerce' or 'e-tailing' – is it worth listening to?

Is it right for your product?

> 66 *My reasoning was that if you can sell it by mail order you can sell it on the Net. It turned out not to be quite as simple as that – but, all the same, it works for me!* 99
> **– Peter Leadbetter, online gardening supplies retailer**

The US online bookstore Amazon is invariably cited as an example of successful selling on the Web. Amazon succeeded by providing a vast catalogue of literally millions of titles at discounted prices, and easy online ordering.

> 66 *Books are an ideal product for selling on the Web. In general, you don't need to handle the product before buying, and an online store like Amazon can offer a vastly bigger range than the local bookshop. In addition books are non-perishable and easy to ship.* 99
> **– Will Forester, Internet marketing consultant**

Statistics indicate that the most popular items for online purchase in these early days of e-commerce are, predictably, computer software and hardware, books and CDs, and travel tickets. But you may be surprised to hear that cars feature up there as well!

How do you decide if your products are suitable for online sales? As Peter Leadbetter says, if you can sell them by mail order you should be able to sell them on the Net. But there are some other important factors to consider.

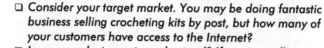

Think . . .

- ❑ *Consider your target market. You may be doing fantastic business selling crocheting kits by post, but how many of your customers have access to the Internet?*
- ❑ *Is your product easy to understand? If you are selling something innovative, unusual, or highly customised which requires pre-sales support from a human being, you might as well carry on taking orders over the phone.*
- ❑ *Selling on the Net means potentially receiving orders from all over the world. Can you handle the shipping? Will the costs be prohibitive? Can you handle foreign currencies? Will you fall foul of customs regulations?*
- ❑ *What about the competition? Selling the top-twenty paperbacks in competition with the megabucks of Amazon could be tough going, but if your product addresses a niche market, or you make it yourself, you can make a virtue of your specialist knowledge.*

Currently over 70% of online shoppers are men, and the typical customer is a highly-paid 30-something white American male. At the moment most products that succeed on the Net are products that men buy (which could explain the existence of online Porsche-buyers!). But this situation won't last – the Web will enter the mainstream just as TV has. In some industries, particularly travel and computer-related fields, the Web may become the obvious place to shop.

> ❝ *Looking at the music industry, for example, we see retail stores with high fixed costs being threatened by Web sites like CDNow. If online stores take even 10% of their business they could be in trouble. In the long run, if you want to stay in business you may have no choice but to go online.* ❞
> **– Will Forester**

Can you afford it?

Two years on, the founder of Amazon, Jeff Bezos, is a millionaire. However, the store has yet to turn a profit! The investment needed to fund the development was substantial, the marketplace is increasingly competitive, and Bezos does not expect to be in the black for a couple of years yet. But he reaped a tremendous advantage by getting to the market first, and establishing the store as *the* place to buy books online.

Of course, your online venture may be somewhat less ambitious, and consequently involve far lower costs. If you sell only a few products, you will not need such sophisticated software.

> **"** *I already had a shop and a merchant account for taking credit cards. When I first started selling online I kept things dead simple, with just a straightforward on-screen order form. I didn't worry about handling payments online, I just processed the credit card orders manually with the terminal I already had, and offered the option of paying by cheque as well. Business wasn't fantastic, but it didn't cost me much either.* **"**
> **– Nicholas Jeffreys, jeweller**

If your Net sales business is a sideline to conventional selling, you can get away with this low-tech approach. But in order to sell seriously on the Net, you need to build your Web site with sales in mind – from the ground up.

Don't assume your existing merchant contract covers you for online selling – check with your bank.

> **"** *I read somewhere that in a good online store you're never more than three clicks away from making a purchase. I've tried to stick to that on our site – every product has an 'Add this to your shopping basket' button to make buying as easy as possible. I put a lot of effort into finding the right software to make this happen.* **"**
> **– Peter Leadbetter**

In addition to the costs of a conventional Web site, you need to consider:

○ *'Shopping cart' software allowing customers to select items and store them in a basket which they will eventually take to the checkout.*
○ *A product database linked to your Web site – you can get away without this facility if you only carry a few products, but if you*

have hundreds it's the only way to ensure that the information online is accurate and up to date.

○ A merchant account for credit cards if you don't already have one.

○ A 'secure server' which encrypts order information. This is essential if you intend to process credit card orders on line. Your customers won't trust you otherwise.

○ A search facility – vital if you carry more than a few items.

○ A system for confirming orders and shipping dates by email.

This sounds daunting, but it is getting increasingly straightforward to create an online shop. Modern e-commerce software lets you set up shop simply by filling in a series of on-screen forms. You can be up and running in a matter of days.

> ❝ *Technically, setting up an online store is easy to do. But, however sophisticated, it won't work without a dose of common sense. You've still got to offer the right product at the right price. Then you have to let your customers know about it. And then you have to deliver it, quickly and cheaply.* ❞
> **– Will Forester**

Look critically at online commerce sites selling similar products and services to yours. Do you feel you could do better?

Selling on the Internet is in its infancy at the moment. This means you have an opportunity to get in on the ground floor and get established before others have started to move. But on the other hand the wounds inflicted by leading-edge technology can be nasty.

Successful e-commerce is all about extracting money from the customer as painlessly as possible. You would be surprised how many online stores make shopping a complicated and awkward procedure.

> ❝ *I decided to do some online shopping to buy my mother a birthday present. I was amazed by the poor design of the first three or four shops I visited. In one of them, I eventually managed to find something I wanted, but when I clicked on the 'order' button I got a message saying 'Sorry, this function isn't available yet'! What's the point of a shop where you can't buy anything?* ❞
> **– Lorraine Marks, freelance financial consultant**

Imagine going into a local supermarket and having to carry all the goods in your arms because there are no trolleys. Arriving at the till, you find it's jammed, and the checkout assistant isn't allowed to take a credit card without a supervisor present. This kind of experience is all too common in online shops.

If you are keen to go ahead, there are basically three approaches:

○ *The service provider you use to host your Web site may offer e-commerce services as an extra. This solution is likely to be relatively expensive, but it means you have a 'one-stop shop'. The provider looks after all the technicalities, and you have one port of call if there are any problems. Obviously you need to feel confident that your provider has the expertise needed.*

○ *Set up shop in an 'online mall', a Web site hosting a collection of shops. Again, some of the work will be done for you and you have the benefit of branding and marketing from the mall owner. This is probably the easiest solution for a small business. However, most online malls have not been an unqualified success – always contact existing merchants before you sign up, to make sure the mall will deliver enough traffic to make it worth while.*

○ *Do it yourself – but be prepared to get your hands dirty! You may have to learn, or hire, technical expertise to get everything up and running. The cost of software, hardware and connectivity for your own server could be very high. On the other hand, you have complete control over the look and feel of your site, and you gain useful skills.*

Consider compromise solutions as well. For example, design and host the Web site yourself and use a third party service to process payments securely. Or you could even find an existing Web store selling goods which are complementary to yours, and rent space in it.

> ❝ *You don't need loads of flashy bells and whistles to have a successful online shop. It's more important to provide easy navigation, ample product information, and easy ways to buy. And small companies can do this just as well as large ones – maybe better!* ❞
> **– Nicholas Jeffreys**

Have you thought of other possible problems?

- ❑ *Can you handle distribution yourself? If not, you need to find a fulfilment company that can meet your needs.*
- ❑ *Think of the practicalities of getting an Internet store to work with your existing business. If you have computer systems for handling orders and stock control, integrating them with a Web store can be a nightmare.*
- ❑ *Don't forget that your staff will need training in this new way of doing business.*

❝ *Selling on the Web is so new, no-one really knows yet what works and what doesn't. This levels the playing field – a tiny start-up company may make a better, more responsive Web site than a mega corporation. Compared to traditional mail order, the start-up cost is small. But believe me, it's hard work!* ❞
– Will Forester

Setting standards

The Internet works because of the existence of standards for transmitting information between computers all over the world. The bad news about electronic commerce is that the standards for handling transactions and payments are still being fought over. So if you are unlucky you could build your site using Betamax technology and then find that the rest of the world is using VHS.

Currently the most widely used standard is SSL (Secure Sockets Layer) which looks after the encryption of credit card details being sent from the customer's computer to your server. However, it does not prove that the customer is who he says he is, or that the credit card account has adequate funds. Relying solely on SSL does not provide an adequate level of security for the merchant or the customer.

❝ *There are far too many cases where merchants use SSL to secure transactions between client and server, but then store the unencrypted information in an insecure location on their server, or transmit it to their distributors using normal email!* ❞
– Andy Toklas

The standard everyone is talking about now is SET (Secure Electronic Transactions). This is intended to address the shortcomings of SSL by providing verification at every stage of the transaction. In essence the procedure is roughly the same as a shop assistant phoning the credit card company for authorisation when you use your credit card. The benefit to the merchant is that, with SET, the bank will guarantee payment, just as it would with a conventional credit card transaction. Other proposed solutions provide even more security by using 'smartcards' with embedded microchips, which require a card reader at the client's end.

There are also various ideas for dealing with 'micropayments' – amounts of money which are too small to justify use of a credit card. These generally take the form of 'electronic wallets' which you can fill up with cash. Although these are very much pilot projects at present, they are worth watching as they could provide a cheaper and simpler way of collecting payments.

> " Technical standard-setting is just a matter of time. There's enough money involved now that the big players will thrash it out between them. In my view a bigger problem at present is getting people to trust the Internet as a place to go shopping. "
> – *Andy Toklas*

Have you shopped on line? What were your feelings as you typed in your credit card number and personal details?

Serious online stores all boast of their 'secure servers'. But do you really feel secure? Not just about the transmission of your card details but about whether the goods will ever arrive, whether your card will be debited with the correct amount, what recourse you have if the retailer doesn't come up with the goods or they are faulty. Most of us don't worry about this when shopping conventionally, or even by mail order. But cyberspace is still an unknown quantity to many people. Unless you are a well-known brand, all they have to judge you by is your Web page. Good design is important – if your page looks sloppy and amateurish, people won't buy.

> ❝ *Always include a page for first-time visitors, clearly signposted from the home page. Explain your security procedures, spell out shipping charges and delivery times. Offer to call them back to take credit card details. Do everything you can to reassure them. And give them a physical address and phone number where they can contact you – it helps to convince them you really exist!* ❞
> **– Peter Leadbetter**

And it's not just the customer who feels insecure. Because SSL currently provides no way of checking the identity of the cardholder, most banks will not guarantee credit card transactions over the Net. The retailer has to take all the risks – which are considerable. Short of actually catching a fraudster in the act of typing in credit card details it is nearly impossible to detect fraud on the Net. This is why some banks won't even give merchant accounts to Internet-only stores. Most online retailers end up either accepting that they will make some losses on dud credit card transactions, or holding the goods until the payment is cleared. This is one of the problems that standards such as SET are intended to address.

In the meantime, it's important to provide as many ways to pay as possible – by cheque or by credit card, via fax, phone, or post, as well as online.

Can you make a go of an Internet-only business?

Many people have seen the Internet as a fantastic opportunity to go it alone and start up their own online business. If you have an email address you are probably accustomed to receiving emails from deranged individuals suggesting you can 'Make $$$$$ FAST on the Internet !!!' without even leaving home. Most of these are pyramid-selling schemes of dubious legality. If you want advice on these, just head for one of the many Web sites or newsgroups promoting them.

On a more serious level, there are ordinary people like you making a living using the Internet. They design Web sites, write CVs, provide secretarial services, sell teddybears, flowers, even cheese! All you need to start is a computer, a modem, imagination, determination – and a lot of hard work. The co-operative spirit of the Internet still rules despite growing commercialisation, and you will find a whole host of other people only too willing to give you advice and support. If you're really strapped for cash you will find many of the resources you need are available for free.

> Low overheads mean you can afford to charge less. Find the right niche and you can genuinely compete on a global level by offering low prices and great customer service.

On the downside, the Net is so new that traditional institutions (such as bank managers) may take a stuffy view of an Internet-only business. Be prepared to shop around to find someone you can work with.

❝ *The fact that start-up costs are so low that you don't have to convince a bank manager is no excuse not to have a realistic business plan at the outset. It could save a lot of grief later.* **❞**
– Will Forester

Successful online selling takes careful preparation

1. Will your product sell on the Internet? Do your homework before you launch.
2. If your only shop front is your Web site, it's even more important that it looks professional and inspires confidence. Take time to get it right before you launch.
3. Find your niche, and use targeted advertising (both on- and off-line) to attract customers.
4. Be nice to your customers! Word-of-mouth recommendations from satisfied customers are the best advertising.
5. If you want to do serious business on the Net, you need to build your Web site with sales in mind.
6. Make it easy for your customers. Don't require them to register or download additional software just to browse through your shop.
7. There are no shop assistants in Web stores. You need to provide enough information for the customer to make a decision, and back it up with a rapid response to queries.

8. Make your pricing policy attractive. Offer discounts or loyalty bonuses to keep customers coming back.
9. Take time to select the right software in order to make shopping as easy as possible.
10. Do everything you can to reassure the customer. Take security seriously, and declare your policy prominently.
11. Let the customer choose how to pay.
12. Invest in your Web site just as you would in a physical shop. Keep it looking smart and up to date – no peeling paint and dust-covered merchandise!

What's in this chapter for you

Assessing your needs
Choosing an Internet access provider
Choosing a Web designer
Maintaining an Internet presence

So, you've decided the benefits of global online marketing are too good to miss. What do you need to get started? This chapter aims to prove that even the smallest budget can stretch to a professional Internet presence. For the more ambitious, it also covers the options at the top end of the scale.

Assessing your needs

Before you start, you need to decide exactly what your access requirements are.

○ Do you have a network? If so, will it handle Internet protocols? (If you don't know what this means, you need a technical expert.)
○ Do you only ever need to access the Internet from the office? Or do your employees need to access it while on the move?
○ Will you need access only occasionally? Or do you need a permanently open connection?
○ Do you have branch offices which also need a connection?
○ Is everyone in the company to have access or just a select few?
○ Do you have in-house technical expertise?
○ Do you require access – and hence technical support – outside normal business hours?
○ Do you need guaranteed availability? Constant engaged tones when you're trying to send a vital email message are life shortening.

 ❝ *Email was seen as a bit of a gimmick to start with. But once people saw how easy and quick it was to use, it snowballed. People even use it to communicate internally, instead of picking up the phone. And after the first three months our fax bill had dropped dramatically!* **❞**
 – Sally Webster, customer service manager

Choosing an Internet access provider

Choose your access provider carefully. If your Internet ventures are successful you will rely on them to keep your business alive, and changing providers can be a major hassle. The criteria are very similar to those you would apply to any key business partner:

○ *Are they well established?*
○ *What is the level of technical support and after-sales service on offer?*
○ *What range of services do they provide? Compare it with your needs analysis – there's no sense in paying for services you don't require, but bear in mind that your needs will change as your business develops.*

If you are intending to develop a Web site to be hosted by your access provider, think also about the following technical issues:

❑ *How big is your site going to be? If it's huge you may have to pay extra for space.*
❑ *How busy will it be? Some suppliers limit the traffic you are allowed and you have to pay extra if you exceed it.*
❑ *What type of site are you going to build – static pages, or interactive ones requiring programming and/or a database connection?*

Exactly what type of connection you need will depend on the size and nature of your company.

○ *If you want to connect a single PC, for sending and receiving email and consulting the Web, a standard phone line and a monthly subscription with an 'Internet Service Provider' (ISP) will suffice.*
○ *If you have a network of (say) five or six computers it is probably more reliable and economic to install an ISDN line and a router (a device which allows all the computers to share the same line).*
○ *A larger company which needs permanent, high-speed access to the Net will probably want to consider a dedicated high-speed leased line.*

You might use more than one of these options: for example, a shared ISDN line at the office, but ordinary phone lines and modems (or even mobile phones) for travelling engineers or the sales force.

ISDN *('Integrated Subscribers Digital Network'): this is a high-speed digital phone line, offering substantially increased speed and bandwidth compared to an ordinary telephone line, enabling you to access more information more quickly.*

Leased line: *a dedicated high-speed telephone line connecting you directly to an access point on the Internet.*

Bandwidth: *the size of the 'pipe' connecting you to the Internet. The bigger it is, the higher the rate of information flow. It is one of the major factors affecting the speed of transmission over the Internet.*

JARGON
buster

New technologies are being introduced all the time in an effort to provide more bandwidth cheaply – satellite, cable, and digital transmission using existing lines. Availability of these newer technologies varies widely.

When choosing your ISP:

☐ *Don't necessarily pick the cheapest. Some of them may be 'here today, gone tomorrow' and/or have poor connectivity to the Internet. Check how long they've been around, and what their user-to-modem ratio is (i.e. how many incoming telephone lines they have compared to the number of subscribers).*
☐ *If you are planning to use your free Web space for commercial purposes, check that this is permitted.*

TIPS

Using an ordinary telephone line

This is the cheapest way of getting connected. Buy yourself a modem, sign up with an ISP, and you are on line. Your ISP will supply you with at least one email address, and usually some free space for setting up a Web site as well. If you just want to dip your toe in the water and get some experience before committing yourself to spending a significant amount of money, this is the way forward. It's also usually the best option for mobile workers.

There is plenty of competition among ISPs at the consumer end of the market so shop around. Buy one of the monthly Internet magazines with listings of ISPs in order to compare prices and offerings, and ask connected friends for recommendations. You can often get a month's free trial on magazine cover disks.

Pros	Cons
Low initial outlay	Your Web page address is likely to be unmemorable (e.g. www.yourprovider.com/homepages/yourcompany)
No need to buy, lease or maintain any special equipment	Performance will be relatively slow
No need to worry about the security of your internal network as you are not connected directly to the Internet	You have limited control over your Web space and probably will not be able to add interactive elements which require programming
A cheap way of getting started	Usually no access to log files for visitor analysis
	It is unlikely to be suitable for connecting your whole company to the Net
	Phone bills can mount rapidly if your employees have open access to the Net
	No service level guarantees

Using ISDN

Many ISPs offer the option of connecting using ISDN instead of a telephone line, sometimes for the same price. This gives you exactly the same services, but a faster, less error-prone connection. ISDN lines pick up and put down the phone instantaneously as it is required so you should spend less time actually connected. This is a more plausible option for connecting a whole network. ISPs will also often offer an ISDN package more suited to businesses, with additional services over and above the standard offering.

Pros

High-speed, reliable connection

Instant connection and disconnection saves time and phone bills

Ideal for connecting a smallish network (say 5 to 50 workstations)

The ISP will often provide and install the necessary hardware

You can if you wish set up your own internal mail server, instead of relying on an ISP for email addresses: useful if you want to give individual addresses to all your staff and use it for internal as well as external communications

Cons

High installation costs. If used extensively, running costs can be high as well

Using a leased line

A leased line gives you total control over the costs, speed, and facilities of your Internet access – for a price! The line is charged at a high flat rate, but there are no phone bills on top.

Pros

High-speed, reliable, and permanent connection

Complete control over costs

With a leased line you become part of the Internet, so you can do your own Web and mail hosting if you wish – no need for an ISP

You can if you wish set up your own internal mail server, instead of relying on an ISP for email addresses: useful if you want to give individual addresses to all your staff and use it for internal as well as external communications

Cons

High installation costs

Security becomes a concern as the company network is now part of the Internet, accessible to anyone with the desire and the knowledge to infiltrate your systems

A higher degree of technical knowledge is required to set up and configure the system. If you don't have it in house, you will need to pay the supplier to do it

What happens if the line goes down? You need 24-hour technical support

If you are at all serious about setting up business on the Internet, you need to establish a 'domain name' for your company – the unique shorthand name such as microsoft.com (sorry, that one's taken!) which is your public identity on the Net. This is simply a matter of registering the name with a naming authority and paying a registration fee plus an annual subscription. Often, your ISP will handle all the formalities for you.

> **Within the limits of availability try to find a name as close to your company name or trademark as possible, to make your address easy to remember.**

Choosing a Web designer

> ❝ *Any fool can create a Web site – and unfortunately many do!* ❞
> **– Andy Toklas, freelance Web designer**

There are hundreds of Web designers out there eager to take your money and create the ultimate all-singing, all-dancing multimedia experience for you. There are a lot of advantages to outsourcing computer-related tasks – you have access to specialist skills without having to worry about hiring more staff, you don't have the day-to-day responsibility for creating and maintaining the site, and you don't have to set aside staff time to do it. Of course, there are disadvantages as well – you still have to spend time specifying and reviewing your requirements, you have less control over the end result, and you must pay for any extra work over and above the original specification. More importantly, you may have to submit ongoing maintenance to the Web designer as well, unless they provide a means of allowing you to do your own updates.

If you have, or can acquire, in-house expertise, it is worth considering the DIY approach. It will almost certainly take longer, but you will develop skills in-house which in the long term will mean you can maintain your site more cost-effectively. It may add interest to an existing staff member's job – you may even discover hidden talents among your team. On the downside, the finer points of creating an effective site that works well for all combinations of computer and browser take a while to learn. Your early attempts could give your corporate image a bit of a knock.

> If you're considering DIY, cost it out in terms of equipment and staff time, and get a quote from a designer as well. This will provide useful information to help you make a decision.

> **❝** *I picked my Web design firm by picking out sites I liked with a similar target market to mine, looking for the designer credits, and then visiting the designers' sites.* **❞**
> **– Lorraine Marks, freelance financial consultant**

Lorraine's approach is an obvious first step in the hunt for a designer. However, there are other points to consider.

○ *Provide a comprehensive brief to your chosen shortlist of firms – this will make it easier to compare quotes.*
○ *Get itemised quotes indicating the cost of Web space (if relevant), the initial design and set-up, and ongoing maintenance.*
○ *Check that the company you choose has enough staff and resources to meet its commitments. If yours is a large or complex project, find out which staff members are going to work on it, and what their experience is.*
○ *Find out names of existing clients, and talk to some of them.*
○ *Set delivery dates, and if possible impose financial penalties for lateness – you don't want to miss a key launch date because your site isn't ready.*
○ *Will the design firm handle promotion as well?*
○ *What are the ongoing maintenance and support arrangements?*
○ *Do you like and respect them? This could be the start of a beautiful relationship!*

> **❝** *The most irritating thing about most of the designers I talked to was that they were only interested in making the site look pretty. In the end I picked someone who saw from the start that the purpose of the design was to market my services, not to show off. She also helped me out a lot with search engines and site promotion in general.* **❞**
> **– Lorraine Marks**

A good designer will take time to understand your business, and will be able to help you create an effective site that meets your objectives. They will need to be able to work alongside your own staff, as some tasks – copywriting or finding appropriate product images, for example – will be your responsibility. So compatibility is important. Biggest is not necessarily best; if you are a small company you might prefer the personal attention and the understanding of your budgetary restrictions you will get from a one- or two-person band. On the other hand, a large database-driven site will probably need the resources of a larger company.

> Arrange regular planning meetings to monitor progress and keep everyone focused on the big picture, not just their own part in it.

Maintaining an Internet presence

So, you're clued-up, on line, and ready to go. Your gleaming new Web site has been rolled out, all your staff have their own email addresses, and you're sitting waiting for the orders to roll in. Unfortunately, all that effort will go to waste if you don't have an ongoing plan to maintain your Internet presence – and a budget to go with it.

> **“** *Planning is the key. If you take the time up front to plan for updating of the site, you can build it into the design, and maintenance will be far cheaper and easier.* **”**
> **– Andy Toklas**

So before you start work, ask yourself some questions. First of all, think about the skills you will need.

> How often will your Web site be updated, and what will the scale of the updates be?

If the site is mainly informational, you will probably be adding new copy, or changing existing pages, on a more-or-less regular basis. Can existing staff do this? What training will they need? How much time will it take?

Site updating

- ❑ *Consider using freelance staff for routine tasks such as typing copy.*
- ❑ *Think about whether you need a system of controls to prevent unauthorised updates to the site.*
- ❑ *If possible, set up a template system so that pages can be updated easily by non-technical staff.*
- ❑ *Make sure you have a reliable backup system, in case of accidents!*

If your site is a large commerce site, the pages may be generated automatically from a database. In this case, someone must be responsible for keeping the database up to date – they may well need specialised skills.

You may decide to outsource all of the site maintenance. But keep an eye on the budget, and compare the cost with what it would cost you to employ someone in-house to do it.

Are you going to maintain a mailing list, for example for a newsletter?

Budget for the time needed to write the copy for the newsletter. Automated software takes much of the work out of maintaining the list itself (adding and removing subscribers, for example) but someone still needs to be responsible for keeping it all running smoothly.

How much traffic do you expect on your Web site? How rapidly will it grow?

This question will probably be difficult to answer at the outset, but you need to monitor statistics carefully and get a feel for the growth rate. More traffic means more business (great!) but it also means more enquiries, and more orders to process. You may need to upgrade computer equipment and hire new staff. With luck growth will be steady, giving you time to adapt.

Do you need to reorganise to handle your Internet business?

66 We were already selling our products by mail order, so at first it didn't seem that selling via the Internet was going to be very different. But we found that Internet purchasers expected answers to enquiries instantly – within hours rather than days. We had to adapt to that by setting up rules for responding to email. Luckily the volume built up slowly, giving us time to make sure all the order-processing staff were fully trained and up-to-speed. 99
– Peter Leadbetter, online gardening supplies retailer

Often, introducing new technology or ways of doing business makes organisational weaknesses which were already there more obvious. Try to forestall this with planning, but be ready to meet unexpected difficulties.

Remember: handling orders and enquiries over the Internet may mean that you need to restructure some departments, and acquire new skills.

Get started

1. Analyse your needs in order to decide on the most cost-effective Internet access.
2. If the Internet is new to you, spend time familiarising yourself with it before launching your own site.

3. Provide a clear and comprehensive brief for work done by third parties such as Web designers.
4. Establish a project team to oversee the development of your Web site.
5. Budget for ongoing maintenance work, and ensure you have enough resources to do it.
6. Integrate your Internet presence into your overall marketing strategy, and reorganise if necessary to do it effectively.
7. Make sure staff whose jobs will be affected are kept fully informed about the project from the start, and that you organise comprehensive training.

With enthusiasm, forward planning, and the tips in this book, you really can launch your business into cyberspace and reach new customers everywhere by using the Internet as a marketing tool!

GOOD LUCK!